T0197401

# Grayson's Story:
# A NICU
# Pandemic Blessing

AuthorHouse™
1663 Liberty Drive
Bloomington, IN 47403
www.authorhouse.com
Phone: 833-262-8899

This book is printed on acid-free paper.

ISBN: 978-1-6655-3170-2 (hc)
ISBN: 978-1-6655-3161-0 (sc)
ISBN: 978-1-6655-3162-7 (e)

Print information available on the last page.

Published by AuthorHouse  07/09/2021

author HOUSE®

Grayson's Story:
# A NICU
## Pandemic Blessing

## CHARNAY PARKS

I would like to thank Children's Hospital, Dallas, for taking exceptional care of my baby boy, and Concord Church, Dallas, for their unwavering support. Special thanks go to my sister, Keondra, for being by my side the entire time. And most especially to Grayson, for being a strong little fighter all through the experience.

My eyes open in a sleepy blur,
I see your face in a glowing haze.
I hear your voice, so soft and sure,
I feel the comfort of your gaze.

My tummy hurts when I try to feed,
I want to tell you how much it aches.
But when I cry, you think I'm in need,
You show you care, whatever it takes

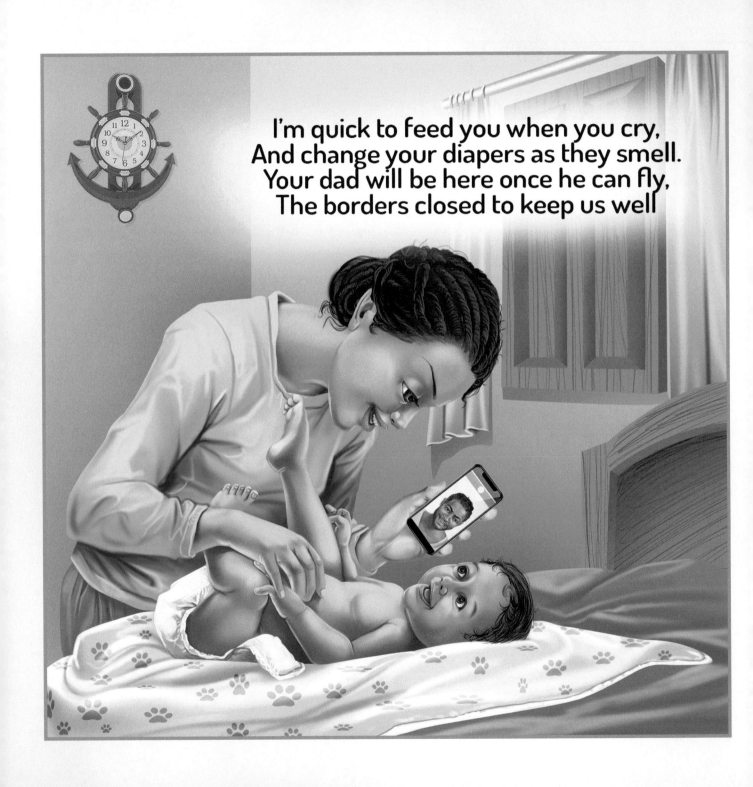

I'm quick to feed you when you cry,
And change your diapers as they smell.
Your dad will be here once he can fly,
The borders closed to keep us well

The pain is one I can bear no more,
I try and try to keep the food down.
When a spew of green covers the floor,
I see your fear as you look around.

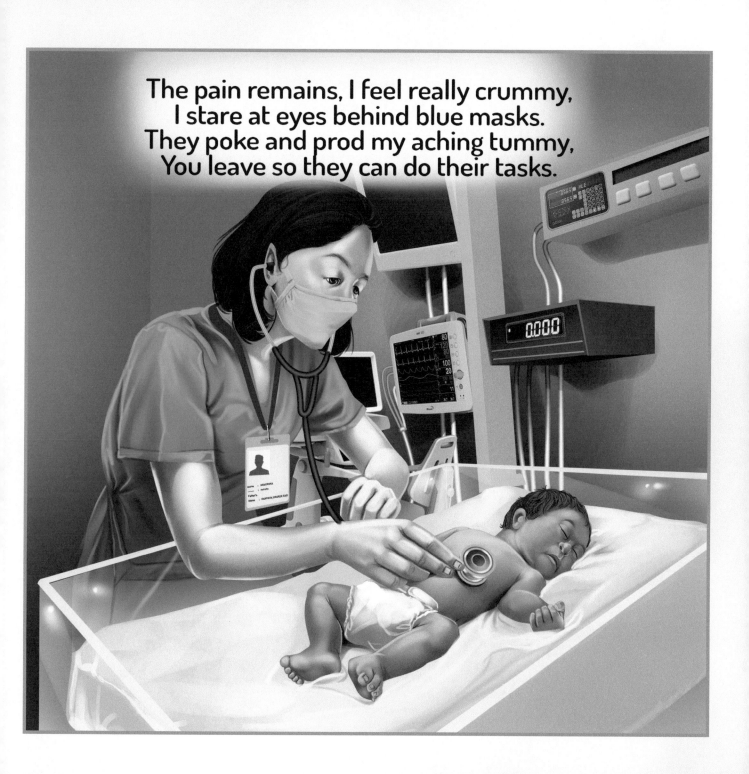

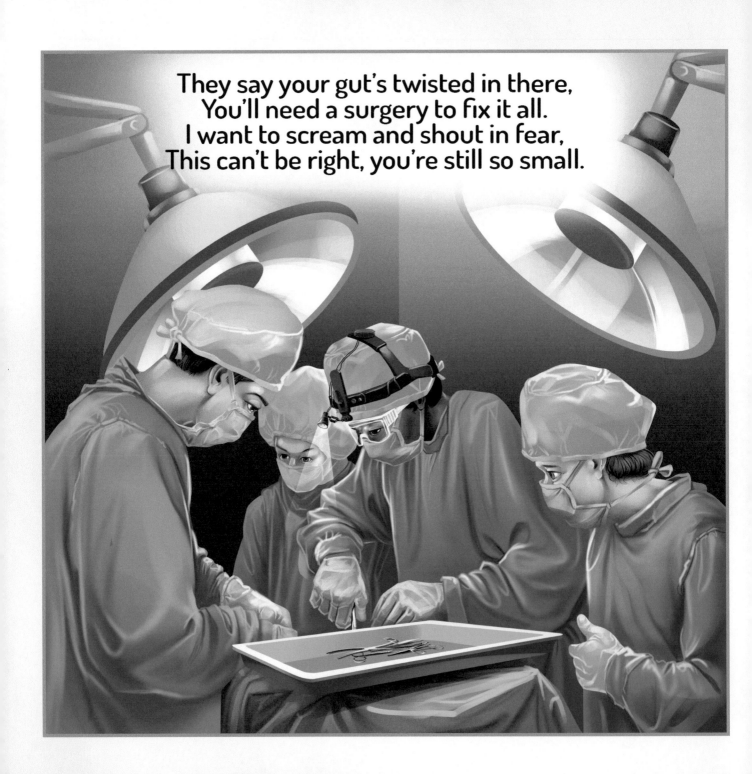

Your surgery starts, I must be strong,
The hours drag on, I wish it was short.
But my sister arrives to give me support.

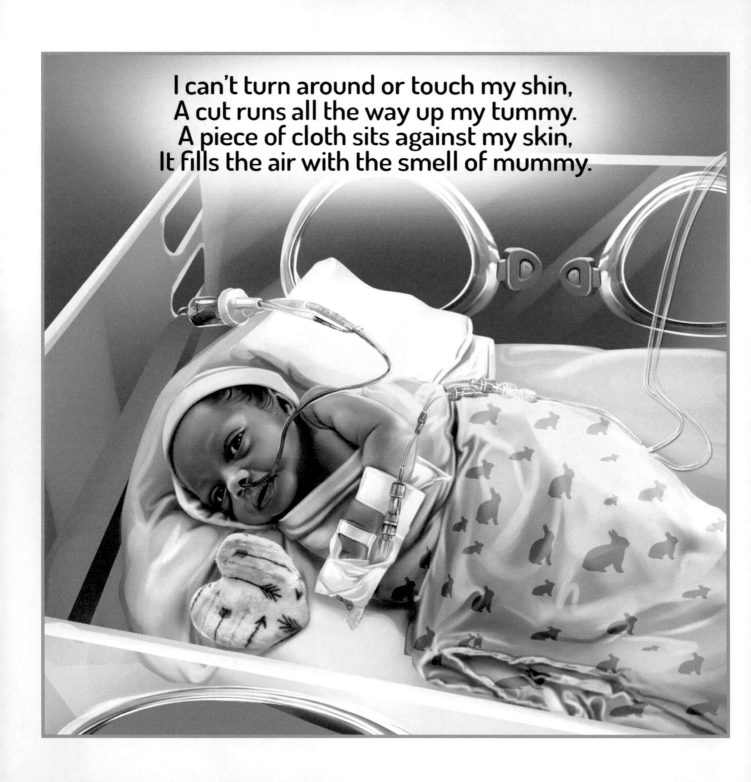

I can't turn around or touch my shin,
A cut runs all the way up my tummy.
A piece of cloth sits against my skin,
It fills the air with the smell of mummy.

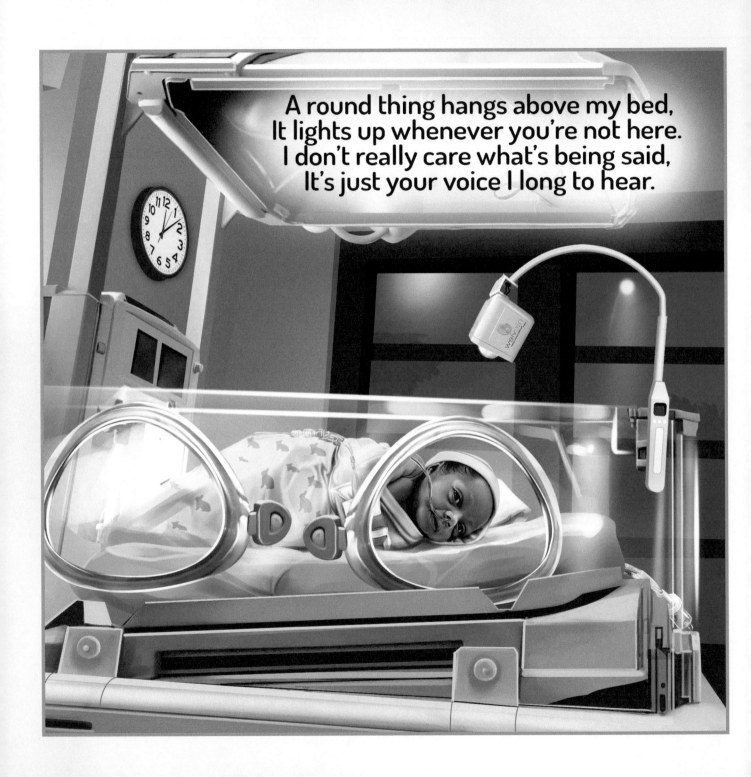

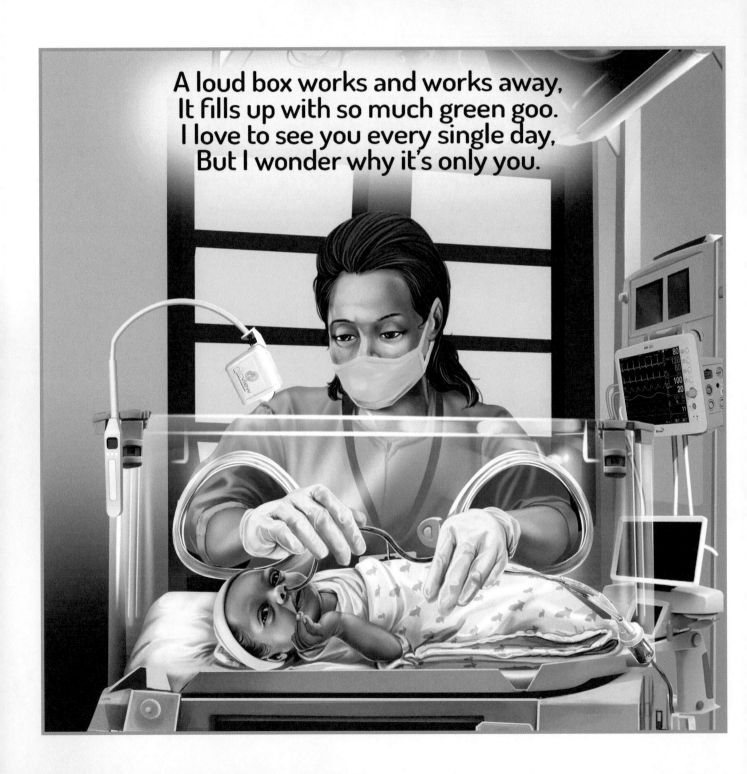

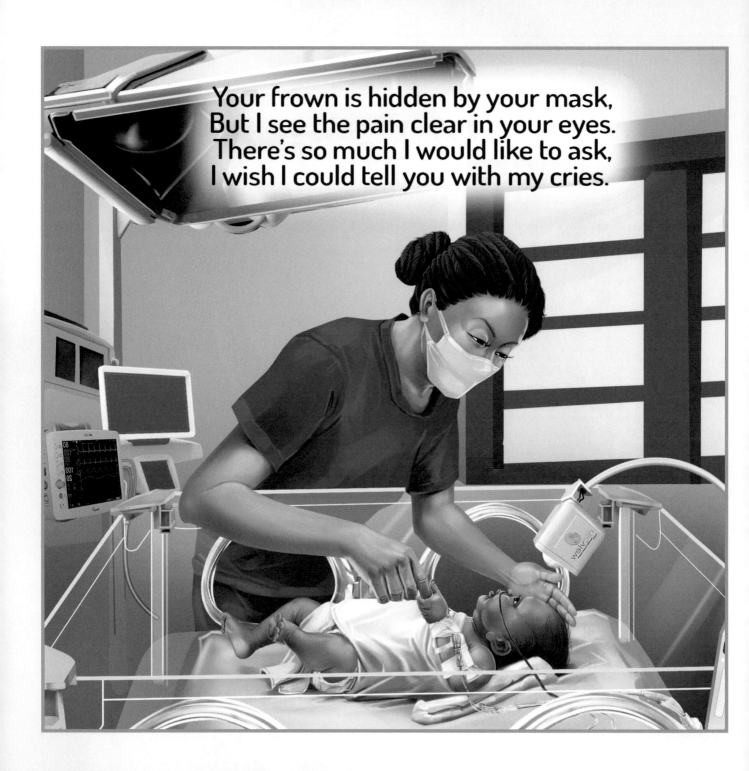

I try to make sure it doesn't show,
But all this stress now takes its toll.
To give him milk to help him grow,
I'll calm my fears and reach my goal.

I pray you'll not catch a cough in here,
I bring warm clothes to show I care.
I speak softly so you can hear,
I give you thoughts of all we'll share.

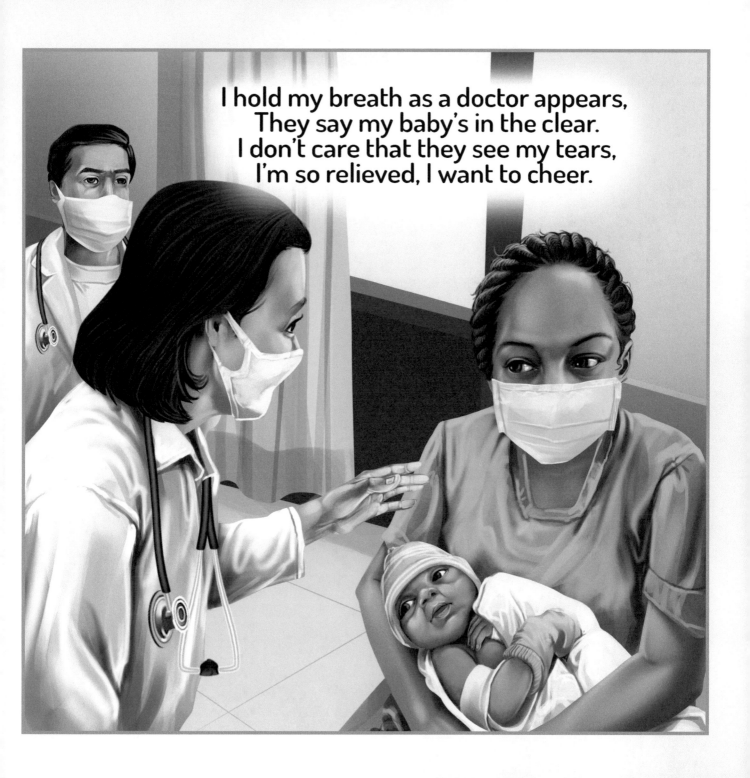

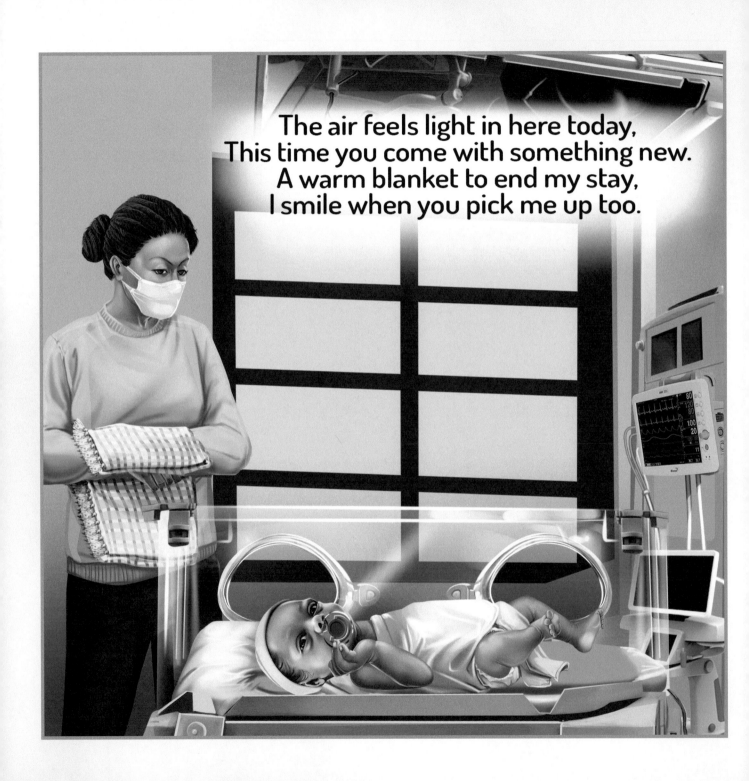

The air feels light in here today,
This time you come with something new.
A warm blanket to end my stay,
I smile when you pick me up too.

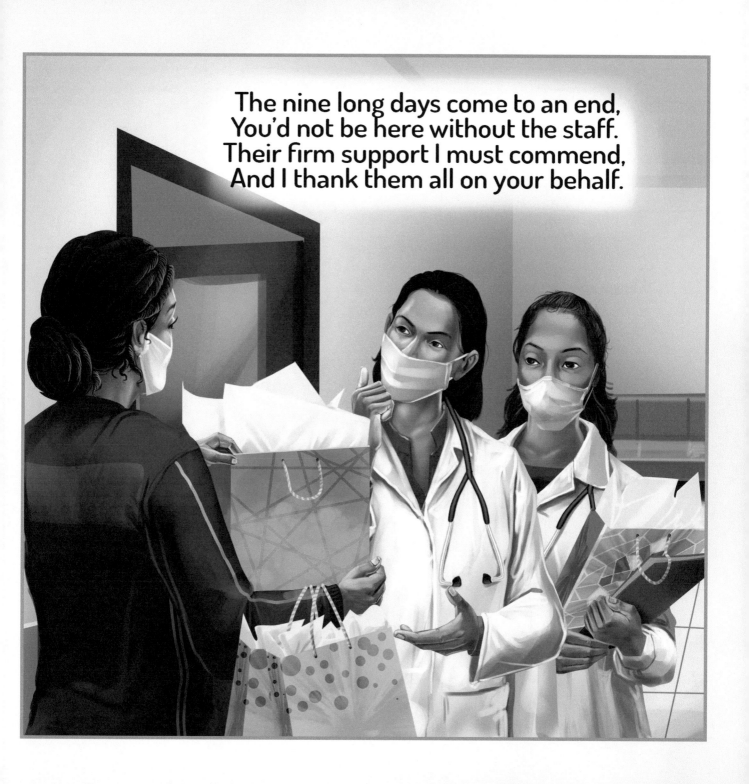

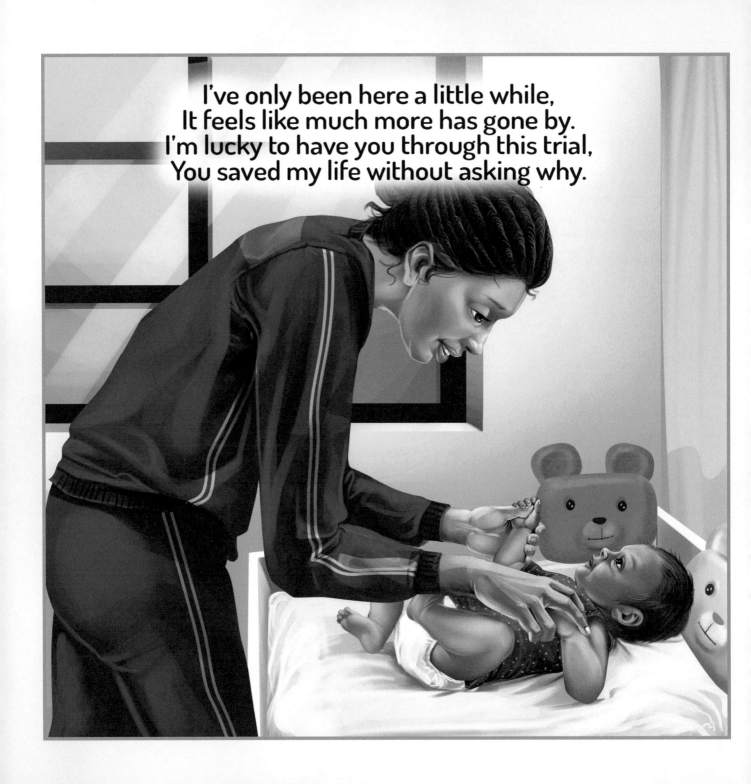

Printed in the United States
by Baker & Taylor Publisher Services